Big Hug Big Kiss

BIG HUG
BIG KISS

How I became a referral
magnet, and you can too

JENNIFER HUGHES HERNANDEZ

Big Hug Big Kiss

Copyright © 2023 by Jennifer Hughes Hernandez

Copies of this book are available at quantity discounts
for bulk purchases.

For more information, contact:

Jennifer Hughes Hernandez
jen.loanwithjen@gmail.com

Printed in the United States of America.

Book Production:
Marvin D. Cloud, mybestseller Publishing Company
marvindcloud@gmail.com

DEDICATION

I dedicate this book to
my late Aunt Marianne Hughes. BHBK
Big Hug Big Kiss

CONTENTS

INTRODUCTION

My first employer was Aunt Marianne. At 12 years old, I would clean her two-bedroom condo every Sunday. Mom would drop me off at 8 a.m. While Aunt Marianne slept, I started in the kitchen, and made my way towards the back of the house until she awakened late in the morning. As she got ready, I would tidy her room, and then, we always finished at Fountain View Cafe for my favorite barbecue chicken sandwich with onion rings. Not to mention the two crisp $20 bills she handed me for dessert. These Sunday encounters lasted for a few years, and the underlying lessons I learned have proved to last a lifetime.

As I grew older, in my late high school years, she would take me on outings and dinners with her colleagues from Coastal States Management. Marianne Hughes was the first woman vice president of a corporation in the oil industry back when it was still a man's world. Aunt Marianne was social, and she knew how to spark immediate conversations with strangers. Within minutes, people would feel they had known her for years. In fact, on the Mercantile Exchange trading floor, her trader ID was BHBK (Big Hug Big Kiss).

Aunt Marianne was my first mentor. As her tag along, I observed how she would network, socialize, and be heard. She definitely commanded attention when she entered the room. Little did I know back then, the skills I was learning from her would lead me to an expansive career as a mortgage loan officer that would span decades. Thousands of referrals have led to financing for families to achieve their dream of owning a home. . Receiving over 1200 referrals annually from family, friends, realtors, and business connections, one could call me a referral magnet.

That's the story I'm about to tell.

CHAPTER 1: WHERE IT ALL STARTED

As soon as I could legally work at age 15, I sought an official job. The years of cleaning Aunt Marianne's house was soon replaced by me being an ice cream scooper, and later a health club receptionist. When I turned 18, I could serve alcohol and my waitressing career began. This would carry me through my high school and my college years. In fact, tips paid my way through an economics degree at Texas A&M University with minimal student loan debt. In the 1990s, that feat was still possible.

Waiting tables prepared me tremendously for what lay ahead. That included handling deadlines, and coordinating food and drinks. Being "in the weeds" (so busy you can't see what's in front of you) was a regular occurrence, and that became my normal. But more than that, my time in restaurants taught me how to engage and service people of all cultures, ages, and economic levels. Everybody eats out at some point. My most profound skill, however, was earning tips. I became an expert. I believe it's because I was genuine and truly cared about each person. For success, it was essential that I impact my guests in a short amount of time. The days of watching Aunt Marianne work the room were paying off!

Sounds familiar? These are all skills necessary in any industry. No matter what your business is , we all have vendors, and we all have clients, whether business to business or consumer! Everyone has to deal with people at some point. That, friends, is what makes the world go around. *If you are looking for more clients and sales, then brush up on your people skills.* Take a course, listen to a podcast, or surround yourself with a mastermind group of the people who are accomplishing the things you seek.

In 1994, I graduated with an economics degree from Texas A&M, and returned to Houston. Living in an apartment with a roommate from college, I continued my waitressing career at a popular Mexican restaurant. I loved to work double shifts for days in a row because the cash tips were addictive. I was in a rhythm, and pretty much on autopilot, until I wasn't. It was late summer, August to be exact, of 1995, and I crashed. At the young age of 24, I had a complete meltdown. Don't get me wrong, nothing is wrong with the restaurant industry, however it was not what I wanted for myself long-term. The late nights and the long hours were exhausting. Ever since I was a young girl, I had imagined being a businesswoman, like Aunt Marianne. What was I doing working double shifts almost every day of the week?

By coincidence, a friend from college had started a mortgage company and was begging me to work for him. He insisted I would make an amazing loan officer. For six months, I brushed him off, and told him he was crazy. I didn't even know how to spell the word mortgage, let alone have any business as a 100% commission sales person.

I have always trusted my gut instinct, and I tend to make quick decisions. Sometimes this can backfire, but up to this point, it has always worked in my favor. This was no different. The day after my meltdown, I called Robert Wagnon and asked if his offer to be a loan officer at his company was still open. "Heck yea!" he said. I started the next day, September 11, 1995. *BHBK*

CHAPTER 2: A NEW BEGINNING

4844
BHBK

My new employer, Robert, was a character. He had always been the life of the party in college, and now was no different. His spirit made people laugh, and he always had a can-do attitude. That resonated with me. He showed me how to befriend people and be comfortable in any size crowd. Robert knew how to work the room. From my earlier days with Aunt Marianne, this was quickly becoming familiar territory for me.

My training was simple. Robert instructed me to open the newspaper to the real estate section and call people. So, I did. In the mid-90s, the internet was unknown. The newspaper was where all the real estate companies advertised. In addition, there were larger quarterly editions with alcaldes for top producers and the like. I called them.

Hi this is Jennifer Hughes (my maiden name), and you don't know me, but I wanted to congratulate you on your amazing accomplishment as top producer this month! I am a loan officer and

I would love to help any of your clients. I'm a hard worker and I can get anything done.

Most of the callers said thank you, and brushed me off. Yet for me, it was getting in the repetition of consistently making phone calls daily, in order to build a habit. Eventually, I modified my script, and as I ventured out to see people, I recognized names, and the connections were piecing together.

Sunday is the biggest day in real estate. REALTORS® showcase their listings in what is called an open house, hoping many buyers will stop by and fall in love with their sellers' beautiful homes! This was a prime opportunity for me to meet REALTORS® because I knew they would be there.

Timing was everything. I waited until there were no cars in front, not wanting to interrupt a prospective buyer walking the house. I always carried a small token of value like a snack, iced tea, or even a quote book I saw at the bookstore. When I arrived, we would chat a bit, I would walk the house, and offer to help sponsor a future open house to bring snacks or lunch. I created value and a reason for them to know me.

The activity that really generated sales was visiting the larger real estate offices with a basket of fruit. I bought apples, bananas, and oranges, and left them in the kitchen for everyone to enjoy. First, it was a way to get past the receptionist. No one turns down food. Second, it was different. *Uncommon.* Most of my competition dropped candy and sugary snacks. The agents loved the healthy fruit! I left a standing flier that had my picture, name and phone number that read, "A Healthy Snack for a Healthy Relationship."

After 18 months of being *consistent,* the phone began to ring. Agents realized I was serious, and a select few of the seasoned agents gave me a chance. That was all I needed. Once I received the referral, I could prove myself.

And prove myself I did. Being a commission salesperson is tough. If you don't close, you don't have a paycheck. In addition to getting the clients, it is imperative to continue to deliver throughout the process. I did this with lots of communication, organization, and follow through.

The other activity I started was sending thank-you notes. Every referral I receive, I write a thank you note to the source. My mom was always a note writer. As a kid, she mandated we write notes to relatives and friends thanking them for the gifts after Christmas and Birthdays. The habit sticks with me to this day. With all the emails and text messages that have become normal in our current day society, taking the time to write a handwritten note sends a special message. *Thank you, Mom!*

To meet more people, I joined a couple of *networking groups*. Texas A&M has an extremely strong alumni group and a great presence in Houston. Every Thursday morning at 6:30 a.m., I went to the City Club, where they met for breakfast. That also was across the street from Aunt Marianne's office at Coastal. I often popped in to say hello. Guess what? She introduced me to her successful friends. Eventually, many would become clients and now repeat clients, even 28 years later.

The other networking group was a commercial real estate association. I wanted to learn more about this segment of the industry, as most of my residential competitors were not focusing on this area. I wondered, how can the commercial and residential sides of real estate collaborate? After many months of *showing up consistently*, the referrals came in.

By my third year as a loan officer, I was having success. My income had surpassed six figures, and I was no longer picking up night shifts at the restaurant. Realtors referred me to their buyers, and to their colleagues in the office. The business people from networking groups were referring others to me as well. In summary, I was generating about 30 referrals a month, which became a solid pipeline of referrals and that kept me active.

These few processes I implemented, became the foundation for a business that would span at least two decades, and is still thriving as I write this book. Networking, consistently writing thank-you notes, and being uncommon. The amazing news is that these are all things you can begin *today* to build the business of your dreams. *BHBK*

Habits you can start today:

Polish your people skills

Thank-you notes

Get in the reps - continuous calling

Join networking groups

Be uncommon (fruit vs candy)

Show up

Be consistent (weekly email)

CHAPTER 3: A STAR IS BORN

Of all the recurring touch points to referral sources and past clients, there is *one* that was and remains my magic pill. I dedicate this chapter to my husband, Fernando, because it was his idea.

In 2002 and 2003, Fernando and I worked together. He left corporate America to help my growing business. Fernando has a degree in industrial engineering, and a master's degree in marketing. I know, an interesting combination. He is disciplined and smart as a whip. Of course, he likes structure and systems, which is what I avoid. Or at least I used to.

Fernando suggested I send a weekly email to my REALTOR® base as a way of keeping in touch. He gave me an example of a large Fortune 500 company that he studied in grad school, and the importance of consistent branding. The key was that I sent it on the same day of the week, with the same subject line, "Interest Rate Update by Jennifer Hernandez." I write about what is going on in the mortgage world that week and send it every Friday at approximately 4p.m.

As I meet industry people at office visits, closings, networking events and seminars, I add them to the email list. At first, I wondered if anyone was opening the email. Then one day, I was in the office of a REALTOR® taking lunch to the group, and someone asked me how my husband did in the triathlon. At first I was wondering, how did they know this?

Then I remembered, he was the topic of my story in last week's Interest Rate Update (IRU)! This was the confirmation I needed to keep going. I was developing an audience and becoming memorable to my sphere.

Back then and to this day, REALTORS® are the largest part of my referral business, because they have immediate access to people looking for homes. For this reason, it has become the area where I focus most of my marketing efforts. In the beginning, I sponsored weekly open houses for brokers, dropped off fruit baskets for everyone to enjoy, and provided valuable information during weekly calls.

Past clientele is another significant source of referrals. I *added a postcard mailer to past clients when the time changes* every spring and fall. Remember, back then there was no internet, so mail was one of the best ways to keep in touch.

I will never forget one year Fernando and I were about to board a plane for Christmas vacation. I received a call from a past client.

"Hi Jennifer, this is Charles. Hey, your marketing really works! I love your postcards when the time changes. I need a loan."

And that was that. It reinforced my suspicion that my efforts were working. Even now, 27 years later, I still mail out those darn postcards when the time changes.

The seeds I had been planting by repetitive processes continued to grow, and my recognition in the industry grew with it. One of my current mentors, Dr. Roy Mason, says that we are always "in a storm, headed for a storm, or leaving a storm." My seas of life were calm, but there were hard decisions looming. I just didn't know it yet. *BHBK*

TAKEAWAYS:

- Identify your referral sources and put in a Customer Relationship Management CRM.

- Send something weekly via email, i.e., a blog, video, market update, or quick tip.

- Send the email on the same day, time, and with the same subject line.

- Send postcard mailers to past clientele two to six times a year.

Scan this QR code and see a sample of my Friday emails.

CHAPTER 4: THE TURNING POINT

In 2002, I was still working for Robert, my initial employer, however the terms changed. While Robert was great at branding and bringing the referrals in, he was not an operational guy. I wanted to be more in control of the day-to-day support. He offered me a branch manager opportunity in which I could run my own show. I was now responsible for all aspects of the loan process and management, like rent, payroll, and packaging the loans to the investors after closing. The corporate name merely provided the backbone of the investor contacts and compliance required to keep loans funding.

Over the next four years, I hired a team of five, which at one point even included my brother, Kenny, my sister, Lori, my husband, Fernando, and even my Aunt Lisa. My experience as a branch owner was not what I expected. Managerial duties consumed my time, not to mention my income went backwards. Being the last person paid was a real drag. Every time I looked up, it seemed payroll had to be processed, the courier bill was due, and the list went on. I hated it. One downside to always having a positive attitude and *glass is half full* mentality, is that I don't give up easily. I make the most of every situation and am slow to call it quits. Although my referrals and closings kept flourishing, on the inside I was slowly deteriorating.

Did I mention that I make quick decisions and go with my gut feeling a lot? I will tolerate things for a while, and then once it hits me, I move, and I move fast. This was exactly what happened one fall day as I was dropping fruit at a real estate office. In the parking lot, I bumped into Darryl, one of my friendly competitors. We never talked much, but had a mutual respect for each other.

Our friendly chit chat turned into 90 minutes of me rattling on about my frustration with the current situation as a branch owner. He was overly receptive, because he had recently become president of a bank owned mortgage company down the street, Patriot Bank Mortgage.

We ended our encounter with a handshake promise that I would see him the next day to ink the agreement to work there as soon as I could unravel my current mess. The first chapter of my 11-year career with Republic State Mortgage was about to take a turn.

Within days, I packed up my office, sold the furniture I could, and put lingering bills payable on my American Express card. The transition was challenging but focused. Unwinding an operation that lasted for four years was mentally exhausting, but I was exhilarated at the thought of a new start. I couldn't wait to return to my true calling, which was networking for referrals and working with buyers. This turned out to be an amazing pivot for me and I soon returned to the true referral magnet that would catapult my business for the next two decades. *BHBK*

TAKEAWAYS:

- Trust your instinct.
- Do what you love.
- If you are miserable, change your situation.

CHAPTER 5: ROCK BOTTOM

4844
BHBK

After starting my new position with Patriot Bank Mortgage, I quickly got back into my zone. I was out more with Realtors®, throwing client parties, and letting the corporate office take care of me. My marching orders were to produce, produce, and produce. That is exactly what I did. On average, 50 referrals a month poured in each. I wrote down each referral's name, phone, and email on bright pink paper to stand out on my desk. This way, everything was in one place, and not scattered in sticky notes all over the place!

At this point in the journey, it's important for me to stop and dig in with you. I need to let you know what worked. *The same systems I had implemented from the first few years were working again.* No magic pill y'all! Let's recap.

- Networking with business groups (I was in at least two at all times)

- Have more than one pillar of business (ex: realtors, business people, past clients)

- Biannual mailers to past clients
- Thank you notes to all of my referral sources each month with a small item of value
- Weekly email to realtors, sent every Friday, with the same subject line
- Quarterly parties for referral sources
- Tracking leads in a database

This, my friends, is the recipe. However, I must give you this warning. The hardest part, just like in your favorite cookie recipe, is that you must have these ingredients, all the time, every time. When you have a little less sugar, or substitute with the low-cal stuff, it won't turn out the same.

Most of you have probably heard about the Mortgage Meltdown of 2008? Thankfully, I had changed companies two years before. Had I been running my branch I likely would not have survived that year. A guardian angel had given me the foresight to make a change in 2006. Now I was working for a company with a super-sized financial statement, and they sheltered me from much of the chaos in those years. I put my head down and kept going.

What most people saw on the outside, though, was crashing on the inside. When I had exited my branch two years before in 2006, I had lingering bills payable. Thank goodness for credit cards, because that is where it all went in the amount of $40,000. Fast forward to the mortgage crisis of 2008. Business was down and my credit card balances kept growing. I thought I would magically have the best month ever, and wipe the debt away. Many months passed, and that magic month never happened.

The time was way overdue to share this news with my husband that our finances were a mess. Up to this point, he did not know. You can probably guess that it didn't go over well. He was furious, and rightfully so. The same guardian angel that had been looking out for me up to this point, was at it again. This time, it thankfully kept Fernando from divorcing me, and implored him to stick around to see me through this mess.

You may think, *Jennifer, what does this have to do with being a referral magnet?* Everything. Because these years, where I crashed and burned, was part of the journey where I experienced something amazing, and changed the course of my life and career forever. *BHBK*

CHAPTER 6: A FRESH START

In the Fall of 2008, a fellow loan officer with our company, Dixie, called a special meeting of the loan officers to meet one of her mentors and coaches, Rick Ruby. I did not know who this guy was, but I respected Dixie, therefore, I showed up. We were 10 around a table in a conference room on the northwest side of town.

This bigger-than-life guy grilled us about our businesses for almost two hours. I was hooked. Never had anyone challenged me like that and told me directly where my blind spots were. He told us about his upcoming biannual seminar, and the cost was $2,500 plus air and hotel. Silently, I gasped for air. *Where would I get that money?* I was right in the middle of the storm with my finances, struggling to pay off the $106K, in credit card debt, and my husband was not talking to me.

Fernando blew up when I asked him to go to this conference that would cost us more than $3,500 after all travel expenses were said and done. Then came the lecture of how spending like this got me into the dilemma we were in right now. He was right. So, I made a deal with him that day. When I pay off the $106K, he would let me go to the next biannual summit of The Core Training. I needed more of that coaching!

In January 2009, another guardian angel moment happened. The interest rates dropped drastically one day. Like a lot. They dropped below 5 percent and the buzz was crazy.

A crucial part of what I am about to tell you has *everything* to do with my weekly Interest Rate Update that is sent every week to over 1,000 real estate agents. The list had been growing exponentially, and included every REALTOR® I had ever met. I was determined to announce the news quickly about this amazing drop in rates! I sent a special edition of the Friday email on Monday. The rates excited and overwhelmed me, and I made a mistake and emailed not only to the REALTORS®, but to every category in my database. Oops! What did I just do?

That one email, distributed to all my past clients, business friends, REALTORS®, and family, kept my phone ringing nonstop. In the span of three days, my assistant, Kenny, and I received over 80 calls from past clients alone to ask about refinancing. I was glad to have Kenny on my team. By 2009, he was solid. The next six months were a blur. We worked constantly to react to the faucet that had turned on from that one email. We worked some nights until 10 p.m. and early days usually started at 5 a.m. Fernando was supportive, of course, because there was a six-digit debt looming over our heads.

Over four months alone, I paid off the entire $106K in debt. *The systems and foundation I had been planting for all those years were being tested, and they worked.* Since I had paid off the debt, I was excited to attend the seminar. A deal was a deal, and Fernando, grudgingly, allowed me to attend the seminar in November 2009.

The seminar for the Core Training was even more than I expected it to be. It is an elite coaching program for top lenders and realtors nationwide. I had finally found my tribe. I don't know how I did it, but I made a deal with Fernando again. If he gave me a chance to sign up for their $2,500 per month coaching, I would make my past financial mistakes up to him.

"Trust your instincts, Intuition doesn't lie."
—Oprah Winfrey

Oprah is right. During the next six months, I graduated from the two-year program. I doubled my income, saved seven figures, and was selected as one of the elite coaches of Core Training.

Over the next decade, from 2012 to 2022, I coached over 230 top producing loan officers all over the country, while growing my team, and developing the business I had only dreamed of. The referral magnetism I had been building had sprouted its wings, and was only just beginning. *BHBK*

TAKEAWAYS

- Trust your instincts.
- Keep planting seeds. (example: weekly email!)

CHAPTER 7: I WISH I KNEW THEN WHAT I KNOW NOW

4844
BHBK

First off, I want to give you the good news. You don't need to work decades to have the business of your dreams. If you are looking forward to generating more leads than you can handle, so you can choose your ideal clients, it's actually right in front of you. This chapter is about the common saying, "I wish I knew then what I know now."

Are you ready for it? Here it is. The missing ingredient is hiring a team to support all those leads you are generating. I don't mean an assistant that you bark orders to. I mean a real team in which there is collaboration, new ideas, and contribution. Depending on your metrics, a team can be you plus one, or two, or ten. As you grow and your plate is beyond full, when you feel scattered and confused most days, that is usually when it is already too late. You needed to hire yesterday.

Having coached over 230 top producing loan officers, I know all the obstacles and objections. I have heard all of them, and I am sure even you are thinking about them right now.

Can I do enough extra business to pay them?

What if I can't make enough to keep them?

Are there enough things to keep them busy?

Will my clients feel passed off?

Will they make mistakes and upset or lose my clients?

How will I find the time to manage someone else? I can't even manage myself.

Where do I find someone? I can't find the right person.

The first thing I will tell you, is what I told my coaching students as they gave endless excuses. It's a bunch of crap. *If you have more leads than you can handle, you have an obligation and responsibility to create leverage.* This leverage will allow you to continue to bless others with whatever your purposeful plan is.

All these fears you have, are keeping you from being a blessing to your clients and your family.

My first child, Diego, was born in 2005. I remember the guilt I felt about hiring a nanny to help take care of him. Would he mistake her for his mother? Would he love her more than me? Deep down, that was my ultimate fear. Hiring Yaya to take care of Diego those first three years until he went to Montessori, was a true blessing. The love she gave him when I was not there was priceless and will always be a special part of his upbringing. Overcoming my fear and embracing the support system allowed me to be a better mom to Diego when I was with him.

In our businesses, it is the same! With the right players on the team, it can create an experience for your clients that you alone could never endure. If you are reading this and you currently have that feeling of overwhelm, please heed my advice.

If you don't know where to begin, look for someone in your sphere to be a mentor. Who do you know who successfully manages a team? Any colleagues? Other branches? Are you part of a mastermind? Can you access an online group on Facebook or Instagram? You could also do what I did and hire a coach to tell you what to do.

I won't profess to tell you leadership is easy. In fact, I will never forget my first real annual team planning.

It was December 2010, and I had been in coaching now for 11 months. My team had morphed from one assistant to four, and my coach told me to have an annual planning session. He even gave me the outline. I thought, *This is great!* This meeting will make me an outstanding leader for sure! I was ecstatic. We booked space at my country club, loaded up an easel and markers, and the first big annual meeting was underway. The outline looked something like this:

1. Introduction/Icebreaker(Game etc.)
2. Team Exercise - Wheel of Life /Goal Setting
3. Review Annual Metrics
4. SWOT ANALYSIS
5. What we need to implement to meet goals next year

As we went through the morning, at least three hours by this point, I wove in commentary from the group. They all gave input as we put ideas on the easel pad. We narrowed down and summarized what we would implement in the coming year.

Kenny, my longest standing team member of seven years, asked me, "Jen, if you knew what you wanted to implement anyway, why did you ask us what we thought?" THUD.

He was right. I had woven all the feedback into the lane I had wanted. I knew the answers to how we would change before the meeting ever started. This was the defining moment I needed to shock myself into further developing myself as a leader. I attended seminars, read books, and listened to podcasts.

I believe this might be the obstacle many people are afraid of, although they can't express it. Before you can work on others, you have to work on yourself. Look in the mirror and realize that attitude reflects leadership. This has been painful, I will admit. At the end of the day, I am the one to blame for errors, lack of systems, a bad customer complaint, or team members quitting.

Ed Mylett says, "On the other side of pain, there is another version of you." Let this be your shining light, leading you toward this lifelong path of learning, growing, and being a light for others. That is what leadership is. Once you start down the path, the rewards are endless, and there is no turning back. *BHBK*

TAKEAWAYS:

- When you have more leads than you can handle – HIRE!
- Commit to learning and growing your leadership skills.

CHAPTER 8: THE SECRET SAUCE

4844
BHBK

Do you ever feel you are gasping for air, or that your to-do list never finishes? How about trying something new and just throwing it out there and hoping it will stick? That is where I was for the first 15 years of my career.

I was having success by accident. Well, let me rephrase that. I had hard work and good intuition on my side. I always did the right thing and kept my promises. That got me far in the beginning. However, at some point, even the best processes can fall flat if not supported by a clearly defined structure.

Before I met Rick Ruby in 2009, I had no one give me real feedback before. The hard kind you hear but don't want to hear, because it might be painful and require something to be given up. Another thing that I know now that I wish I knew then, is that *the most significant things in life are the ones that make you uncomfortable.*

Do you want to know what one of the simplest things I implemented my first week of coaching that made the largest impact? Scheduling calls. That's right. Sounds simple, right? Well, why had I not done that for 15 years? When someone calls, emails or texts you, offer them appointment times to schedule a 15-minute call.

For example, "Hi Mary, thank you so much for reaching out at John's recommendation! Let's have an introductory call. It takes about 10-15 minutes, and then we can determine the next steps for your situation after that. Does 10 a.m., 12:15 p.m. or 4 p.m. work for you today?" Rinse and repeat.

Scheduling calls, using a calendar, having daily team meetings, and one on one coaching my growing team every 30 days are some ways I built a new foundation. What I realized is that none of these things, not one, was a big new idea. They were things I knew. I needed someone to show me where my blind spots were. If I could achieve my goals faster, and have more fun doing it, why would I not go for it? *I knew I had to invest at the level I expected results.* I could not wing it anymore. It was time to surround myself with people who were where I wanted to be.

Whether it's a coach for fitness, business, or your finances, the result is the same. Accountability and structure will help you get to the next level, as long as you do the work! You are probably thinking, *when you are starting in business, money is tight.* I understand the struggle because I started with nothing but a college degree and a telephone.

I can only imagine where I would be today if I had heard this advice at the early start of my career. Find a mastermind, a podcast you can follow, or a local group you can join.

The missing ingredient in all those years that I did those basic systems for my business was coaching.

This, my friends, is the secret sauce. It is the key to becoming a referral magnet that will become the foundation of a career. I think back to all the times I went into things alone, being the pioneer and figuring it out all on my own. The moment in 2010 that I signed up with the Core Training, I literally saw results within three months. I already had some basics down before I started coaching. I made sure I was coachable and implemented what the coach told me. My business and I exploded. *BHBK*

I have a gift for you should you be interested in weekly motivation that will spark ideas to grow your business. Scan the QR code below to subscribe to my weekly business tips that are released every Tuesday.

TAKEAWAYS:

- The most significant things will make you uncomfortable.

- Invest at the level you expect results.

- Hire a coach.

CHAPTER 9: EVERYBODY NEEDS A WINGMAN

My story would not be complete without giving honor to the importance of a wingman. Or wingwoman. Or wingperson. You catch my drift. There are two people who have played crucial roles in my journey, and without them, I would be lost.

The first is my husband, Fernando. We married in my third year of business, as I was growing exponentially. The tolerance, the patience, the sacrifice, and the love he has shown me all these years are invaluable. He has been my cheerleader and biggest fan behind the scenes and without him, I'm not sure I could have had the endurance to accomplish all that I have.

Once we had our first son in 2005 and our second in 2010, Fernando took charge like never before. He willfully wants to clear my plate of anything and everything so that I have a clear head and get into my business mojo every morning.

My favorite story to tell about Fernando is how he will wake up in the morning and when I ask him what his day looks like, he simply replies, "Whatever you have for me. What can I do for you today?" He is a dream come true, and I am so blessed to have him as my life partner!

Your personal wingperson doesn't have to be a spouse or partner. If you don't have one of those, I fully suggest you get a housekeeper or house manager. This is someone who can run errands, help with personal things, or even pay bills. As your business grows, you need to have a reliable person to take things off your plate.

The second wingperson everyone needs is at the office. In July 2003, I hired my baby brother to be my assistant. The mortgage industry was in the middle of a refi boom, and on my own I was closing 25-30 loans per month. It was nuts, and I was beyond overwhelmed and clearly needed to hire, and fast.

My brother, Kenny, still lived in Tennessee after college, and was working for a large national bank. He knew how to view credit and calculate debt to income ratio. These are the basics that we use in mortgage. In addition, I wanted him home in Houston where we grew up.

It took some convincing, but finally he and his cat, Biggio, came home. His first day of working with me was July 1, 2003. As I write this book, he recently celebrated the 20-year anniversary of being on my team! He is dependable, consistent, protective, loyal, supportive, and committed. His daily support, compounded, has allowed me to focus on client acquisition while he handles the operations behind the scenes. We complement each other perfectly.

Your future wingperson doesn't have to be with you for 20 years either. The value of having a dependable and committed person at your side, who can handle those tasks that are not your strengths, is priceless. It will unlock a treasure chest of capacity, attention, and care for your clients like you have never seen.

The hiring of team members was the genuine connection that had been missing. It linked my marketing processes and the delivery of promises together. When you become excellent at what you do, your plate gets full quickly and without notice. Adding team members expands your capacity and helps shift your business from transactional to relational, and the referral magnetism you were meant to release comes front and center. *BHBK*

CHAPTER 10: RINSE AND REPEAT

4844
BHBK

As we close our time together, thank you for choosing to spend time with me and read about my journey. My hope for you is that you have a basic understanding of the key components of a thriving business, and that you go out into the world and create your own greatness.

We all have our strengths and differences. *Find out what yours are.* Find what you are passionate about and what brings you joy. When you identify them, be sure you fill your day with those things, and that your wingperson is doing the other things you don't like or are not good at.

I know in the beginning of a business, money is tight, but in today's reality there are part timers and virtual assistants that can do just about anything! Blending your processes, hiring a coach, and having a team will create an amazing recipe.

The rinse and repeat concept is the real thing. Whenever I deviate from the simple structure of my recipe (aka process) and begin adding a bit of this and that, guess what? Things get over complicated, and I end up returning to the basics. Life never ceases to amaze me that all things *simple* are usually the right answer.

You have blessings to give to this world, and by holding back, you are keeping those blessings hidden. The world needs you to contribute and flourish so that you can help make yours a better place! Big Hug and Big Kiss to you and your journey. I would love to hear about your accomplishments.

You can email me at jen.loanwithjen@gmail.com or follow any of my social media and drop me a note @loanwithjen *BHBK*